Christia and Feminism

Sonya J Wratten

St Marks CRC Press Sheffield

Together in Hope

Resources for

Christian Faith Today

This series of resource books is the result of a number of
organisations working together to give encouragement
and hope to those who seek a credible Christian faith
for the twenty first century.

We hope that these books will be helpful to those individuals
and groups, inside and outside of the Church, who are
exploring matters of faith and belief.

We are grateful to our authors and encourage others
to offer their services.

For further information about the sponsoring
organisations please see the back cover. If you wish to
contact the editorial group,
email: **togetherinhope.editor@gmail.com**

The current convenor is Adrian Alker

The books in this series can be bought via the PCN Britain and
Modern Church websites (see back cover)
or telephone 0845 345 1909.

Printed on recycled paper by Pickards.org.uk Sheffield (0114 275 7222)

Sonya J Wratten

Sonya J Wratten has been a trustee of PCN Britain for three years and is currently Priest in Charge of All Saints, Bedford. Previously to ordination she trained as a Community Artist in the realm of community drama and has worked as a Community Development Worker in the urban context with churches and other faith groups. Sonya's interests lie in interfaith dialogue and community engagement, faith and the arts and of course, feminism! Sonya has been a feminist as long as she can remember, believing that the goal of gender equality is one of our most important, unfinished tasks in an increasingly culturally and religiously diverse context.

I would particularly like to thank Alan Race for reading drafts of this booklet and for his understanding. To be understood by another is a blessing indeed. This booklet is dedicated to my family who have always encouraged my self-development and to the many people who continue in the pursuit of gender equality, including the coming generation who are taking us into the next wave of feminism.

It is also important to note that two of the most influential and ground-breaking books regarding Christianity and feminism were published in 1983: 'In Memory of Her' by Elisabeth Schussler Fiorenza and 'Sexism and God-talk' by Rosemary Radford Ruether. 2013 was the 30th anniversary of the publication of these books and the questions they raised have retained a strong resonance today.

Sonia J Wratten

Christianity
and Feminism

Contents

Introduction

What does it mean to be a woman in 21st century Britain? As people who seek to make sense of the Christian faith with contemporary thinking, this booklet explores some of the issues of feminism today and what a credible progressive Christian feminist theology might look like in the light of such reflection.

In recent times we have seen a restored interest in feminist discussion as a result of populist books such as '50 Shades of Grey'[1] and 'How To Be A Woman'[2], which have dominated the bookshelves of Waterstones and Tesco. Some might also remember a surge in feminist discussion in the 1990s when the post feminist rhetoric of Helen Fielding hit the bookshelves in her comical but troubling tale of the single mid 30s diarist, Bridget Jones[3]. These popular cultural examples have become catalysts for discussion on what it means to be a woman today, often cited as third wave feminism or post feminism.

In addition to examples of popular culture, there has been an increased awareness of gender related atrocities and violence globally against women. Examples such as the shooting of 14 year old Malala Yousafzai for championing educational rights for young women in Pakistan and the gang rape and murder of an Indian medical student within two months of one another in 2012[4] have sparked resurgence in feminist debate on the international stage. Most Christians will have a desire to respond to such events and topical debates but in order to do this we need to consider what a progressive Christian feminist theology looks like. This booklet aims to assist readers to look briefly at the relationship Christianity has had with the development of feminism, what shape feminist theology has taken in the present time and what the progressive directions of the future might be in terms of furthering radical theology in this area. With these components in mind this booklet is divided into the following three chapters:

1. Where we've come from: Radical Female Roots

2. Where we are: Contemporary Christa Understanding

3. Where we're going: Progressive Directions

---

1 James, E L 50 Shades of Grey (London: Arrow Books)

2 Moran, Caitlin How To Be A Woman, (London, Edbury Publishing, 2011)

3 Fielding, H Bridget Jones's Diary (Picador, 1996)

4 Malala Yousafzai shot in the Swat valley, Pakistan October 2012 and medical student fatally gang raped in Delhi, India December 2012.

The theological sources of scripture and tradition, reason and experience are used in this booklet to encourage a model of theological reflection which draws on our personal experiences and those in the world around us. The arts, popular culture and media also give us indications of contemporary issues relating to gender inequality. This booklet uses such examples in order to find out what some of the pertinent issues of feminism are today.

There are questions to prompt the reader(s) to consider their own experiences for individual study and /or group discussion. Exploring radical and progressive responses to an array of subjects in Christian theology is one of the main objectives of the 'Together in Hope' series. But, rather than beginning with the contemporary, this booklet firstly looks at some of the radical roots of the church's relationship to female culture in the Christian tradition, moving on to rediscover the feminist theologies of forbears such as Rosemary Radford Ruether. Reaffirming such *'Ruetheresque'* theology in this booklet is essential, for its intrinsic radicalism remains foundational for all later developments.

In terms of furthering theological reflection on issues of feminism and gender inequality, a great deal of the future lies in interfaith dialogue because of the increasingly multicultural makeup of society and because the global has become local. This is therefore a topic that I touch upon in the third chapter but it could easily be a whole second volume, as it takes feminist theology to a further level of progressiveness. It is also very much part of my own experience as a woman ministering, living and working alongside others from different faith traditions.

Although this booklet focuses in the main on Christian feminist theology, it must be noted that the subject and pursuit of gender equality is much broader than this. It is hoped that this booklet will inspire us to think critically about one strand of gender equality: feminism and its relationship with the Christian faith. But it is important to state that equality issues related to men and transgender individuals are also significantly important matters to pursue under the gender equality banner.

Issues surrounding faith and feminism have always been an important part of my life and each of us have had our own journeys, struggles and experiences which have been shaped by the generation into which we have been born and the environments in which we grew up. Someone once asked me what is most important to me as a woman, and I replied 'to be a thinking woman'. That is something for which women still make huge sacrifices.

Despite the focus of this booklet being on feminism, the core issue of faith and gender is about enabling all people to be equal and, through this, fully human. In our desire and action for full humanity for all, we bring about God in the world.

Questions:

1. When you hear the word feminism how do you react?

2. What images does the word feminism conjure up for you?

3. What is your initial understanding of the relationship between feminism and Christianity?

---

1. Where we've come from: Radical Female Christian Roots

If you, like me, love a good period drama then you'll know that many classic novels such as 'Vanity Fair', 'Howards End', Jane Eyre' and 'Tess of the d'Urbervilles' (to name but a few) all raise questions about the role of women at home and in society in the periods in which they are set. In the films 'The Duchess'[5] and 'Anna Karenina'[6] issues related to female sexuality dominate the thread of content in these two stories. Culturally accepted as permissible for husbands to have extra marital affairs (driven by their perceived, alpha male desires) these attitudes are turned on their head when it is the heroines who cave in to such desires.

Caught up in adulterous entanglements these female protagonists have to choose between their home, children and their lover when a day of reckoning comes. The adulterous husbands, however, apologise to any offended parties and carry on in status and lifestyle as if nothing had ever happened. The women lose everything because of their promiscuity and the men retain everything.

The well-known book, 'Tess of the d'Ubervilles', speaks of similar attitudes towards female sexuality and the ownership of women's bodies by men as landowners and husbands. Tess finds herself a 'wronged woman' when she is raped by the master of the estate for whom she works. She gets pregnant as a result, the baby dies and Tess has to baptise the illegitimate child because the parish priest refuses to do so. When she anxiously tells her new husband of her past (knowing that to be an impure bride was culturally unacceptable in Victorian England) he abandons her, even though he had also confessed to not being a virgin on their wedding night. For the man to be impure is one thing but for the woman to have had previous sexual liaisons (even in the case of rape) was deemed an abomination and intolerable.

In the light of the historical context reflected in these novels, one might be surprised to learn that historically the church has been far more influential and radical in forwarding the rights of women than we might first give it credit for. There has always been (and hopefully always will be) a radical side of the church that has sought to be subversive and prophetic in raising its head above the institutional parapet and proclaiming 'this is not how we authentically interpret the Christian faith'. As with such movements, the radical and

5   2008, Directed by Saul Dibb
6   2012, Directed by Joe Wright

prophetic church has often paid a high price for its subversive tones against its own institutional leadership and those institutions in wider society with which the church may have colluded.

The next section looks at some historical examples of the prophetic and radical church with regard to feminism.

Prophecy and Order

'Christianity, although absorbing earlier and contemporary misogyny, was a potent force for liberation. It revolutionized relations between the sexes and contributed the idea of spiritual equality among human beings...'[7]

As with many stories of human emancipation, the journey of feminism and its relationship with Christianity has been an ever volatile one. It could be said that Christianity has been both friend and foe to what has been termed, from the 20th century onwards, the feminist movement. As Monica Furlong states, 'Woman is the best friend religion ever had, but religion is not the best friend woman ever had'.[8]

Rosemary Radford Ruether differentiates between the radical church and the established religious order as the *Spirit-filled Community* and *Historical Institution*[9], noting that tension between these two sections of the church has been continuous throughout Christian history. The historical institution or order of the church reflects the social and political hierarchical nature of established society and the structured church body. In contrast to the order of the church is the Spirit-filled Community. The Spirit-filled Community or radical part of the church is that which seeks to break down such hierarchies and enable a prophetic voice to come through.

Another way of understanding this might be to think of the church having two sections: one which is about structure, order and establishment which keeps the traditions of the past prominent and the other section being the radical and prophetic. This latter part of the church seeks to listen to contemporary society, apply reason to their understanding and move faith forward in the world.

A wise teacher once said to me, when I was on the cusp of ordination, that each of us in the church belongs to one part of the church: *prophecy* or *order* and that it is impossible to truly belong to both!

---

7   LeGates, M *In Their Time: A History of Feminism in Western Society* (New York, Routledge, 2001) p.27.

8   Furlong, M Mirror to the Church: Reflections on Sexism (London, SPCK, 1988) p.1.

9   Radford Ruether, R Women – *Church: Theology and Practice* (New York, Harper and Row, 1988) p.11.

If you are interested in radical and progressive Christian theology then you, like me, will probably gravitate towards the former. You may have even left the church because you think the prophetic side is not strong or loud enough in the present time. With regard to the development of feminism the prophetic side of the church has assisted in the development of feminist thought and action (both faith based and secular) and we shall refer to some historical examples of Christian feminist heroines in this chapter.

Questions:

1. **How do you view the idea of there being two sections in the church: prophecy and order?**

2. **Reflect upon your own experience(s) of Christianity and feminism looking at situations where this subject may have arisen.**

Heroines of History

How far back the actual movement of feminism itself goes is debatable. LeGates states[10] that even in the Middle Ages, where feminist orientated heroines within Christendom can be found, it was a minority female culture asserting itself, rather than a feminist movement per se.

Female culture distinguished itself in the Middle Ages through women finding opportunities for public expression in religious piety. The only official roles for women in the church existed in religious communities. These communities however were not just for pious, religiously devoted individuals but also served as an alternative place for women who wanted (or were forced by their families) to escape the expectations of matrimony and motherhood.

Although these communities were commonly held under the spiritual and financial authority of male monks and priests, there were some exceptions where women devotees held complete authority over their religious community. It was through these more radical religious communities that women found a level of autonomy that was rarely found anywhere in the Western world at that time.

10 LeGates, M ibid p.51.

The Beguine movement was such a community, unusual because it had in place autonomous female leadership and it was not exclusive to women from privileged social classes. They actively sought to encourage urban, working class women to be part of their community as well. The Beguines were radical and inclusive because of these factors but they paid the price and had eventually to break from the church because of suspicions from the established order of the church over their all-female leadership.

Amongst the individual married women who found opportunities to be released from domestic patriarchal structures in order to discern a Christian ministry, Margery Kempe's story is a remarkable one. A married woman who mothered thirteen children, Margery struck a deal with her husband that if he agreed to abstain from sexual intercourse, she in return would eat with him on a Friday (when she normally fasted) and pay off his debts. Margery wanted to use her new found freedom, away from the obligations of marriage and motherhood, to explore what she discerned as a religious calling.

Kempe is a rare example in this period of someone who defied domestic male patriarchy in order to explore her religious vocation. Known personally to Julian of Norwich, Kempe's pilgrimages took her as far as Jerusalem and Constantinople. For a married woman with thirteen children that was quite an achievement in the 15th century. Kempe is also hailed as writing possibly the first autobiography in the English language entitled 'The Book of Margery Kempe', which details her pilgrimages and growing devotional relationship with God.

The Quaker movement also shone out at the radical end of the church, encouraging women who felt a religious vocation to leave their domestic responsibilities as mothers and wives to become travelling preachers across Europe and North America. Led by Margery Fell, the married women preachers were actively encouraged to pursue their religious vocations even if their husbands disagreed, qualifying them as women who were way ahead of their time around the 17th century.

A great deal is owed to the Quaker movement for their encouragement of women preachers. Often the achievements of women in history are easily forgotten but the influences of the first female Quaker preachers are noted clearly in Diarmaid MacCulloch's 'A History of Christianity'[11]. In their immigration to North America,

11 MacCulloch, D A History of Christianity (London, Allen Lane 2009) p.723

Quakers were martyred for their progressive theology and beliefs. Both men and women suffered flogging and even had their ears cropped, with four Quakers being hanged in Massachusetts in the mid 17th century for missionary activities. One of those hanged was a woman named Mary Dyer[12] who was a preacher and is now remembered as one of the four 'Boston Martyrs'.

Another courageous and radical woman Quaker was Anne Hutchinson. A preacher and spiritual advisor, she campaigned for civil liberties and religious toleration in puritan-run Massachusetts until she was sent into exile and excommunicated. Statues of Anne and Mary stand in Boston today to commemorate their courage at a time when women were understood to be of so much less value than men.

A further prominent female figure who found a way to assert herself in the course of Christian history was Josephine Butler. A privileged woman married to a clergyman, Josephine used her social status to campaign for the health and wellbeing of women, particularly those on the margins of society such as sex workers. She was most notably remembered for her ruthless campaign against The Contagious Diseases Act, which Josephine believed discriminated against some of the most vulnerable women in Victorian England. The Act was supported by many powerful men in the higher echelons of society including church leaders. Josephine and other women however, were successfully assertive in campaigning against the Act, highlighting the subjugating attitudes of men towards women at that time.

It is clear in these stories (in times of an emerging assertion of female culture) that the heroines in question dwelt in the prophetic and radical part of the church, often with costly consequences. A great deal is owed to women such as these who not only desired to make the lives of disadvantaged women better but also asserted themselves in overwhelming patriarchal societies. It is through such stories that we can see the radical part of the church at work and there are many other examples that reveal how feminism has radical roots in the church.

Questions:
1. Can you think of other figures in Christian history, who you think have been prophetic and radical in their time?
2. Which figures of history have influenced you in your life?
3. Who do you think are the progressive and prophetic voices of Christianity or of feminism today?

12 ibid, p.273

Christianity:
Influencing the First and Second Waves of Feminism

Christianity clearly had some influence on the beginnings of feminism in western society, even if it was not what we would now label as feminism. Both prophetic groups and individuals found opportunities to express themselves as leaders, preachers, mystics and social reformers in a male-led world. These developments took place through the prophetic, Spirit-filled and radical parts of the church and Christian communities.

So huge was the influence of this prophetic and radical side of the church, many feminist writers believe that feminist theologies of the Christian tradition have entwined their roots with secular women's campaign groups of the first and second waves of feminism in the 19th and 20th centuries.[13] This is something for the progressive church to celebrate proudly. It is a history which is all too frequently forgotten when reports of church misogyny cloud our view and it reveals how influential the radical and prophetic arms of the church can be in transforming society.

Where the first wave of feminism of the late 19th and early 20th centuries had concentrated on the achievement of equal civil rights, such as women gaining the vote, the second wave of feminism was a new phase in feminist discussion. If the first wave of feminism conjures up images of protesting suffragettes, second wave feminism was concerned in the main with the rhetoric of how women were viewed and talked about in the home and the world around them. This period of 20th century feminism might make you think of burning bras and the public defacing of sexually suggestive images of women. More significantly, however, second wave feminism concentrated on topics such as gender bias language, the subjugation of women's bodies and the criticism of men being perceived as the superior sex. This prompted religious as well as secular discussion on woman's 'default position' as the inferior sex, with feminists making the world aware that women were understood normatively as the *object* and men the *subject* and that, more pointedly, this was no longer acceptable.

Regarding the focus of second wave feminism, Mary Stott says 'It is a search for an identity as a human being, a deeply felt, often inarticulate, protest at being typecast by sex from birth to death.'[14]

13 Fletcher Hill, J in Hedges P and Race, A Eds., *Christian Approaches to Other Faiths* (SCM Press 2008) p.136.
14 Stott, M *'The Women's Lib Movement is a Search for Meaningful Identity'* in Cochrane K Ed Women of the Revolution: Forty Years of Feminism (London, Guardian Books 2012) p. 3.

These discussions came to light in Europe and North America through key texts by feminist intellectuals such as Simone de Beauvoir[15], Betty Friedman[16] and Germaine Greer[17] and at a similar time in the Christian tradition through the work of theologians such as Rosemary Radford Ruether and Elizabeth Schussler Fiorenza, whose work we will look at in more detail in this chapter.

Questions:

1. **How do you think people in wider society view the relationship between Christianity and feminism?**

2. **How realistic is it to be able to be radical and prophetic regarding gender issues in the church?**

3. **If you could change one thing in the present time regarding women and the church what would it be?**

Reconstruction: The Forgotten Gender

In this booklet we have already gathered examples of women who have been agents of history within the Christian tradition, but sourcing stories of such women has not always been easy. A greater consciousness of women's presence and influence in the shaping of Christianity came about in the late twentieth century due to what is termed Reconstructive Theology, led by theologians such as Rosemary Radford Ruether and Elizabeth Schussler Fiorenza. In 1983, Ruether and Fiorenza each published a ground-breaking book: 'Sexism and God-Talk'[18] and 'In Memory of Her'[19] respectively.

It cannot not be underestimated how influential these books have been in shaping and developing Christian feminist theology on an academic as well as practical basis. Such texts have helped pave the way for developments in women's ministry by constructing legitimate arguments for the spiritual equality of women inside and outside the church walls.

One of the main concerns of Reconstruction Theology was to unearth stories of women in Christian history that had been overshadowed by those of men. It was identified by theologians such

15 de Beauvoir, S *The Second Sex* (Middlesex, Penguin 1972)
16 Friedman, B *The Feminine Mystique* (London, Penguin, 1963)
17 Greer, G *The Female Eunuch* (London, MacGibbon and Kee Ltd 1970)
18 Radford Ruether, R *Sexism and God-Talk* (London, SCM 1983)
19 Schussler Fiorenza, E In Memory of Her (London, SCM 1983)

as Ruether that woman had lost their stake in the story of Christianity because of a focus in the main on men. This convinced her that in order for women's stories to be told and for Christianity to be a faith for women as well, theology needed to be re-shaped, re-thought and reconstructed in order for women's voices, stories and interpretations to be heard.

Questions:

1. Do you agree or disagree that women's stories can or have been lost in history?

2. What is your knowledge of the influences of women in Christian faith and practice? Eg. Who immediately springs to mind when you think of famous writers, theologians etc.

3. What is your impression of the Bible regarding women?

Restoring Women to History and History to Women

The title of the book 'In Memory of Her' was inspired by the unnamed woman in Mark's gospel who anoints Jesus:

'And truly I say to you, wherever the gospel is preached in the whole world, what she has done will be told in memory of her.'[20]

There have been many women who have played a significant role in the course of history but whose contribution has been unrecognised and unacknowledged due to the preference, often unconsciously, of man's contribution over and above that of woman when both have played a part in the shaping of history. In the book 'Good Wives?'[21] Margaret Forster tells the story of three women and their life journeys alongside well-known husbands. She seeks to unearth the stories of women such as Jenny Lee (wife of Aneurin Bevan and a promising politician in her own right) and Mary Livingstone (wife of missionary and explorer David Livingstone). She writes from a biographical perspective, trying to reclaim their voice and reconstruct history by allowing the stories of these women to be told rather than just those of their husbands.

However it seems that times are potentially changing regarding the perceived role of the wife alongside the famous, powerful husband. In the recent TV series 'The Politician's Husband'[22] traditional gender

20 Mark 14: 9, NRSV
21 Forster, M Good Wives? (Chatto and Windus 2001)
22 Milne, P The Politician's Husband shown on BBC 2 in 2013

16

placing is turned on its head when the wife and 'back bencher' MP character replaces her cabinet minister husband after his resignation due to a conflict with another senior minister. This lead female character takes over from her husband as the prominent person throughout their lives: domestically, professionally and even personally when sexual prowess is explored in the bedroom as part their own on-going power struggle. The woman is 'on top' in all ways, becoming in this story the *subject* rather than the *object*.

Thinking about how women have been portrayed in the bible is a key part of reclaiming women in Christian history. It was not simply Elisabeth Schussler Fiorenza's aim to recover the significance of female figures in biblical books but also to find a way for women to be upheld and promoted through biblical analysis without compromising on the interpretative model of historical criticism; this was called 'Feminist Critical Hermeneutics'[23]. In other words, Fiorenza sought to find a way in which women could be vindicated in biblical discussion without making up history and trying to stay true to the historical context of the Bible. In the words of Fiorenza, she wanted to 'restore women to history and history to women.'[24]

Before the work of Fiorenza there was a group of women in 19th century North America who had already highlighted the problem of biblical interpretation being used to advocate misogyny and patriarchy in society. 'The Women's Bible'[25], written by Elizabeth Cady Stanton, is a political tract which sought to fight against the dominant maleness of biblical interpretation and it's usage in furthering the oppression of women at that time. Because Elizabeth Cady Stanton felt that women were so badly treated through Christian teaching she refused to even attend suffragists' prayer meetings where prayer and bible readings were used.

Cady Stanton argued that the bible was written as male inspired and not God inspired because it was written by men, was used for the advancement of men and furthered the oppression of women by portraying women as thoroughly unequal to men.

It might be difficult for us now to imagine a time when the God of the Bible was not understood in the Christian tradition as siding with the oppressed but this thinking in the Christian tradition emerged through liberative theologies being developed such as Liberation Theology, Feminist Theology and Black Theology. In 19th century North America and England there was a growing consciousness of

23 Schussler Fiorenza, E In Memory of Her (London, SCM 1983), p.1
24 Schussler Fiorenza, E ibid p.4
25 Cady Stanton, E The Women's Bible (1895, 1898)

women's emancipation but it was still a very male dominated society and this was very much supported by biblical teaching. Elizabeth Cady Stanton and her peers were therefore true Christian progressives of the day in their protest that the bible was being used to further oppress them.

Questions:

1. Do you think it is possible to interpret the bible as a liberative resource for women?

2. Do you think women and men read and interpret the bible differently?

2. Where we are: Contemporary Christa Understanding

'Christa' is the central concept in Nicola Slee's 2011 book 'Seeking the Risen Christa'[26]. On the front cover there is a painting of a vibrant table scene, with a woman dressed in red at the centre and three men gathered around her. The scene is joyful and celebratory, easily interpreted as a Eucharistic scene with the female Christ figure, the Christa, at the heart of it.

In the film 'Babette's Feast'[27] one might also interpret the leading character Babette as an illustration of a female Christ figure. Set in 19th century Denmark, Babette is a French refugee taken in by two sisters who lead a church community in a remote, rural setting. Babette, unbeknownst to them, was a high ranking chef in Paris but fell on hard times when her husband and son were killed. When Babette has a surprise lottery win she asks the sisters if they will allow her to cook a lavish meal for the church community in celebration of the anniversary of their late father, a much revered and sombre leader of the faith.

As simple people who hold a puritanical approach to Christian living, they are concerned about dining in such luxury but do not want to discourage Babette in her desire to share her windfall with them. At a church council meeting one evening they discuss this dilemma and decide that they shall allow Babette to cook for them but once the food and wine passes their lips they will simply pretend to themselves that it is the most basic of foods, determined not to be seduced by it.

As the evening draws on, the more good wine they drink and the more exquisite food they taste, the more relaxed, joyful and open they become. The puritanical community laugh with one another, open their hearts to one another and celebrate the goodness of life in the sharing of one another's company. It becomes clear that by using her culinary talents, kindness and love for these people Babette has become their gatherer in drawing the community together to sit at the table with one another, break bread and become one body. She is the Jesus-like servant and liberator, freeing them from their stifling puritanical ways and enabling them to live as fully as possible for that one night and hopefully beyond as well. Babette could be seen in this as the female Christ figure, the Christa at the table.

---

26 Slee, N *Seeking the Risen Christa* (SPCK 2011)
27 1987, Directed by Gabriel Axel

In the previous chapter we looked at Reconstruction feminist theology from a biblical perspective, which recognised that women of history in the Christian tradition needed to be reclaimed and new models of biblical interpretation developed. This chapter moves us on to discover how Reconstruction and the development of feminist theology paved the way for understanding the concept of Christ more inclusively, namely Christ as woman.

Task:
If you have access to the internet, search for 'female Christ' to see the variety of images that appear.

Questions:
What do you think about these images of a female Christ?

Christ as Woman

'Christa' the 1975 bronze sculpture by Edwina Sandys was the first widely known female depiction of a female Christ and it has since inspired many similar depictions up to the present day. A little while ago I posted one of these images on my Facebook page and even though such pictures are not unusual, this picture sparked a surprising amount of debate and strong reaction. The picture provoked online conversations between Facebook followers about the usefulness of such an image, ultimately asking the question: if Jesus was a man then why do we need depictions of a female Christ? A counter question and one which has become prominent in Christian feminist discussion since the 1980s is: Can a male saviour save woman?

It is widely accepted that as a person of history Jesus was a Jewish man from first century Palestine. The symbolic figure of Jesus as the Christ however has signified much more than him simply being a human figure of religious history. It is in the Christological understanding of Jesus that feminist theology holds much of its debate. If we take the view that in Jesus we encounter something of God (encompassing within this a broad spectrum of Christological interpretations) then the maleness of Jesus fuses with the symbol of 'Christ' which merges in turn with our image of God. This christological understanding whereby the maleness of the symbol of 'Christ' became central was established early, consolidated with the emergence of Christendom onwards and largely went unchallenged until the Enlightenment period.

If we understand the Christ figure as someone who points us towards God or embodies God (depending on your theology) then it is a male Godhead that Christian history and tradition has put forward. If the image of God is therefore one which is clothed in maleness this is, as Nicola Slee states, hugely problematic: 'The major problem for feminists is that, in the doctrine of Jesus as Christ, a male human being is identified uniquely with the person and activity of God.'[28]

The question facing progressive Christians is: 'who is Christ in progressive theology?' But in order to consider the place of Christ or rather Christa when thinking about feminism then we need to look briefly at the argument for the depiction of a female Christ. We must consider what Christ or Christa can say to the world about our desire for gender equality. If Christology is traditionally perceived as proclaiming Christ as saviour, then it is essential for us to ask what kind of saviour is Christ for women?

Questions:
1. What is your understanding of the Christ figure and what does it mean to you as a progressive Christian?

2. Do you think that a male Christ is inclusive of all peoples or do you think that a female Christ (Christa) is useful?

Radford Ruether's Reconstruction of Christ

In order to learn how Christ was reconstructed and became woman, we need to firstly understand why the maleness of Christ was so important historically. From Christendom onwards Christian orthodox belief has upheld the maleness of Christ which has led to the dominance of a male Christology. This took hold at a time when the Christian faith moved from being a marginal Jewish sect to the established faith of the Roman Empire. Male dominated Christology was being expounded in mainstream Christian belief. But this male focussed understanding of Christ has not gone unchallenged. Alongside the growth of gender consciousness in the latter 20th century in the secular feminist movements there was also the watershed reconstruction work of Radford Ruether from the 1980s onwards.

28 Slee, N Faith and Feminism (London, Darton, Longman and Todd 2003) p. 49

Radford Ruether focussed more on the doctrinal side of Christian theology and as we looked at previously, Elisabeth Schussler Fiorenza on biblical reconstruction. In her landmark book 'Sexism and God-Talk'[29] Radford Ruether begins by detailing the history of mainstream Christological thought, beginning with an exploration of Jewish messianic hope in the early days of Christianity. This Judeo-Christian understanding of Christ was recalibrated after the Council of Chalcedon in the 5th century when the notion of a male dominating Christology took hold. As Christianity entered the mainstream, the character of the church also changed with its new imperial status: As Radford Reuther says

'Just as the Logos of God governs the cosmos, so the Christian Roman Emperor, together with the Christian Church, governs the political universe; masters govern slaves and men govern women.'[30]

With this newly acquired imperial reign of the church, Christ became the ruler of the Empire's 'new world order'[31] with the philosophy attached to such governance that male leadership (divine and human) was understood as the norm and this has lasted until the modern period.

'The possession of male genitalia becomes the essential prerequisite for representing Christ, who is the disclosure of the male God.'

With such doctrine lasting for so many years (and still to this day) one can understand the challenge Ruether and her contemporaries had in reconstructing a Christology that reflected alternatives which embraced the liberation of women through the symbol of Christ.

Questions:

1. **How do you connect with the figure or symbol of a male Christ?**

2. **Do you think that different depictions of Christ assist people to engage further with the Christian faith and feel more included?**

---

29 Radford Ruether, R Sexism and God-Talk: Towards a Feminist Theology (London, SCM Press 1983)
30 Radford Ruether, R ibid p.125
31 ibid

Diverse Experiences of Woman

Feminist theology has expanded since the heyday of the late 1980s and has been shaped into more specific cultural and social groupings. These include the following global expressions but this list is not exhaustive:

Womanist – Black feminist theology

Mujerista – Hispanic feminist theology

Minjung – Korean feminist theology

One critique of feminist theology of the past is that it has been locked in ivory towers of elite academia, dominated by white middle class women and this was one of the criticisms of 'The Women's Bible' and secular suffragist movements in the first wave of feminism. But one hopes that feminist theology has been broadened now by the experience of a wider variety of women from different cultures, sexual orientations, race and social class.

To understand this broadening of Christian feminist theology further it might be useful to look at some reflections and poetry from Christian women of different backgrounds and experience:

1. An African American Reflection on 'The Colour Purple' By Alice Walker[32]

Reflecting on Alice Walker's novel an internet commentator notes the gradual realisation within one of the female African American characters that for the figure Jesus to be empowering she needs to see him in a different light:

'She realises that the God she needs is not the one she originally envisages. It is significant that she sees him as white and old "like some white man work at the bank." All the angels are white too and she comes to realise that this God is useless to her. Nettie's letters begin to show her that Jesus was more like her than a white man "with hair like lamb's wool", not "white" at all.'

2. A Christa Collect[33] for Stephen

'Christa, born among us as the poorest black baby,
surviving disease, malnutrition, illiteracy,
war, flood and drought,
enduring the world's repeated indignities:
come, show us your power,
overturn the structures of injustice that murder and maim,
render all our idolatries void.'

32 http://www.litnotes.co.uk/color.htm
33 Slee, N Seeking the Risen Christa,(SPCK 2011) p.148

3. Fat Christa[34] *for Lisa Isherwood*

'In praise of her amplitude
Her huge breasts that suckle children
Resting on the belly rolls she's given up trying to hide
Her arms and legs as tree trunks
that have stood in the forest for centuries.
In praise of her enormous body wide as a world
diffused in the dimpled flesh of the earth
folds and ripples of rolling fields
mounds that are hillocks,
tors and mountains (her breasts)
cavernous underground caves (her womb)
and dark running waters (her blood)
the heaving heat of her constantly beating heart.'

4. A Mujerista Reflection[35]

'A mujerista is one who struggles to liberate herself, who is consecrated by God as proclaimer of the hope of her people. Mujerista is one who knows how to be faithful to the task of making justice and peace flourish, who opts for God's cause and the law of love.

In the mujerista God revindicates the divine image and likeness of women. The mujerista is called to gestate new women and men: a strong people. Mujeristas are anointed by God as servants, prophets and witnesses of redemption. Mujeristas will echo God's reconciling love; their song will be a two-edged sword, and they will proclaim the gospel of liberation.'

Questions:
What is your response to these reflections of various women's experiences of the Christian faith?

---

34 Slee, N, ibid p.141
35 Ada Maria Isasi-Diaz http://telling-secrets.blogspot.co.uk/2012/05/ada-maria-isasi-diaz-two-edged-song.html

3. Where we're going: Progressive Directions

In this final chapter we will look specifically at some of the issues facing women today, highlighted in examples from the media and culture. We will also identify two elements of current social action within the wider feminist debate, looking at how progressive Christians could get involved in such projects and where opportunities for response might be possible.

Experiences of Women Today

'Women's Hour' on BBC Radio 4[36] produced a list of the 100 most powerful women in the world. These included lawyers, pop stars, entrepreneurs and scientists to name but a few. One may agree or disagree with the selection of women that were chosen but one thing such a list reveals is a desire to nominate role models in our society and state where women have got to in terms of breaking through the glass ceiling in the workplace. Of course, as many feminist writers pointed out recently in the build-up to and aftermath of Margaret Thatcher's funeral, just because such a powerful woman smashed through the glass ceiling in the male dominated world of politics this does not make her a feminist, unless it can be argued that she helped others to do the same.

It is generally agreed that the role models presented to us through culture and media have a great influence on where we are today or where we have yet to reach in terms of gender equality. In order to learn about the pertinent issues affecting women today one can learn a great deal from the culture around us. Reflecting on culture alongside our convictions of faith is sometimes referred to as correlation theology. This model of reflection means that our starting point is to look at the world and identify what is happening, what issues are important in people's lives in families, communities and places of work and then use this information in our subsequent theological reflections.

Popular culture in particular can be a way in which to learn what is 'pushing people's buttons' in the present time. The theologian Paul Tillich stated that we should not dismiss the culture of our time if we are truly to learn as theologians about the present human condition:

36 http://www.bbc.co.uk/programmes/b007qlvb/features/power-list

'The theologian is bound to attend to such cultural specifics in order to understand how in each generation the generic existential issues are articulated.'[37]

More recent theologians from the discipline of cultural theory believe popular culture to be a source of unification, which can speak of shared experience in socially, religiously and culturally diverse situations. A piece of popular culture, such as the book '50 Shades of Grey', might prompt us as theologians to ask why so many women have purchased this book and look at the discussions that have taken place (on Facebook, Twitter and book review sites) following its publication and mass popularity. This book has sold over 5 million copies in the UK so far and is some say, more popular now than the 'Highway Code'! It must therefore tell us something about society today as a source of *shared experience* that has stimulated dialogue between people who might not otherwise have anything else in common.

In 2011 another popular book was published, which cut to the heart of populist feminist discussion, entitled 'How To Be A Woman' by Caitlin Moran. In her autobiography of her life from early childhood to her present thirty-something years, she gives a humorous account of the main stages of her life so far (family, school, career, marriage), whilst weaving in a potted history of 20th and 21st century feminism and the influence of this on her as a young woman. In December 2012 'How To Be A Woman' won the public vote for the Galaxy Book of the Year awards, after dominating book charts since its release in the summer of 2011. Reviews from women journalists as well as the public have hailed it as a witty discussion on what it is to be a woman in UK post-feminist society today.

In discussing 'How To Be A Woman' with a small but diverse group of female friends, colleagues, family members and acquaintances, I discovered that there was a shared sense of continuing sexism in society, experienced by this group and raised in this book. Therefore a shared experience of a present day issue affecting women had been revealed through the medium of popular culture. Not only is this an effective way in which to identify some of the pertinent issues of the day affecting women but it can also be used as a source of solidarity within increasingly diverse and plural societies.

37 Graham, E, Walton, H and Ward, F, Theological Reflection: Methods, (London: SCM Press, 2005) p115

26

Present Day Christas

One of the most shocking stories to hit the headlines in recent times was the Taliban shooting of 14 year old Malala Yousafzai for championing education for girls in the Swat Valley, Pakistan. Now a Nobel Peace Prize nominee, the impact of her story, recovery and subsequent campaigning has brought the issue of gender discrimination and the continuing denial of basic human rights for some women in the world to the international stage. As someone who has worked in a community that is mainly Muslim my interpretation of this situation is that she is a present day Christa because of the context in which I live and work. You may have your own examples of such women and men who live out a costly faith in order to bring about further gender equality in the world.

One only needs to type Malala's name into an internet search engine to learn how widely followed her story has become. Even though this happened many miles away, the speed of our media feeds, ensure that we become embroiled in epic injustices such as this. Because we are so aware of such events through access to instantaneous media coverage, stories such as this become part of our global picture, as well as part of the feminist narrative of the day. Access to such stories is good news for feminism because it makes us aware of the plethora of feminist related issues across the world.

The development of social media (Facebook, Twitter, internet chat sites etc.) has connected us personally to the lives of individuals and communities who we might not otherwise come into contact with. It brings the stories and journeys of others thousands of miles away into our living rooms, coffee shops and places of work as never before. A positive element of this is the opportunity to campaign effectively and easily by signing online petitions that make their way around the world from England to Ecuador and Chile to China!

A good example of one piece of global social action that has been happening since the gang rape and murder of the Indian medical student in New Delhi, January 2013, is the 'One Billion Rising' campaign. Focussed around a central website[38], groups of women (secular and religious) have been mobilised to gather together in their local towns and cities to raise awareness about violence against women globally. These gatherings have included parties, street demonstrations and arts based workshops. If you want to know where God is at work in the world you only need to look at the website to get an idea and it is something that as progressive Christians we should be supporting and hopefully finding ways to respond to as well.

If you have been reading and listening to the news over the last twelve months you may have noticed that there has been a resurgence in awareness of violence against women on a national as well as global scale. This is not to say that violence against women has lessened in recent times or necessarily increased (there may be statistics to argue either way) but the fact that people appear to be increasingly more intolerant of this on a global scale is a very positive thing indeed. It seems as though there is a global value that states any violence against women is not to be tolerated and this is surely something to celebrate.

Despite such positive moves in attitude generally against women being violated in the domestic or work environments, this is still a huge issue both at home and abroad. As I write, several well-known women journalists have undergone abuse via Twitter in connection with the recent successful campaign to add the writer Jane Austen to sterling bank notes. The level of abuse that these women were sent on their smart phones was astounding and highlights the fact that we still have a raging, misogynous thread in our society.

Another sign of hope in the wider world that speaks of the younger generations being mobilised to continue campaigning for gender equality, is the newly formed 'Feminista' group. After marching at Westminster in 2012, dressed as suffragists from previous periods of feminism, these young women feel called to continue campaigning for equal rights for women in the UK. Issues such as affordable child care and the banning of page 3 models in tabloid newspapers are among their goals. This is not just social justice in action but the raising of consciousness afresh in the next generation regarding feminism. Again, this is something we, as progressive Christians, can respond to either through the use of the internet

38 www.onebillionrising.org

(joining in with online discussions etc.) or participating in their events.

More than anything, these examples of present day feminism give us an understanding of where the Christa is (the symbol of the suffering, liberated and resurrected woman) and what the issues of the present day are for women globally. Let the following verse from a poem by Nicola Slee be an effective challenge to us:

'Why is the Christa always suffering, broken, dying?

Where is the risen Christa?

Why have we not realized her?

Is she still on her way to us?

How can we help her arrive?'[39]

Questions:

1. **To what extent are you aware of contemporary violence against women and what is your response?**

2. **How do Christians campaign and respond to issues such as violence and abuse?**

3. **In your own experiences do you think that we are globally less tolerant of any violence against women or is there just more exposure to such situations?**

The Need for Interfaith Dialogue

We have noted from the stories above that issues regarding gender equality and feminism are hugely diverse as the world becomes smaller and the global becomes the local. This means that our own feminist discussion encapsulates not only on-going sexist issues, such as breaking through glass ceilings in the workplace, but also the issues of those with whom we share this world, our Muslim sister Malala being such an example.

In order to work together in eradicating gender related injustices and atrocities we have to understand one another religiously and as well as culturally. Mutual respect, trust and understanding can be fostered through interfaith dialogue as well as the sharing of one another's experiences about what it means to be a woman today.

39 Slee, N Seeking the Risen Christa (London: SPCK 2011)

In a recent article[40] the journalist Tanya Gold spoke of secular feminism losing its way because it seemed as though there is nothing left of any substance to fight for, that although Western feminism has conquered many things it has now become virtually irrelevant. If Tanya means here that patriarchy has been in principle defeated and that we are now in a period of consolidation then I would agree. On the other hand if she means that there are only small changes to bring about practically then I would disagree strongly. It is clear from the stories that we read about in our internet news feeds, televisions and newspapers that there are many who need support in bringing about an equal position for them as members of the human race. Interfaith dialogue in the context of feminist theology encourages a sense of mutual accountability for one another, beginning with the ideal that 'one woman's problem is every woman's problem'.

We live in an increasingly religiously and culturally diverse society. It is important for us to reach out beyond our own faith traditions and learn about the context of others particularly if we are to join together in bringing about gender equality for all.

40 'More than a spare Rib', The Guardian, 29/4/2013

Conclusion:

How To Get Involved: Campaign Websites and Resources

It is apt that this booklet concludes with information on how progressive Christians might take action regarding issues of feminism and gender equality. In this booklet we have looked at the roots of feminist theology in the Christian tradition and how this has influenced and overlapped with that of secular feminist movements. We have looked at some of the core influences and developments of Christian feminist theology although we have not looked at them all and there are many more people who have helped pave the way for an emergence of this particular theological school of thought.

We have also looked at how culture and media play a part in telling us what the issues are for today's women and how we might find a sense of shared experience through our discussions and dialogue. We have also noted the need for interfaith dialogue in our on-going thinking and action regarding issues of feminism in the hope that we will go beyond our own immediate contexts and join with others in a common cause for gender equality, if we have not done so already.

Below are some useful contacts and resources but this list is not exhaustive as there are many projects and worthwhile campaigns to become involved with.

1.   38 Degrees: People, Power, Change

A petition and campaign website. You can sign up to receive online petitions via email and Facebook. There are many which involve issues regarding gender equality.

www.38degrees.org.uk

2.   One Billion Rising

Campaigning to stop violence against women

An internet based campaign group that gathers people together for demonstrations, campaigns etc on a local basis to stop violence against women.

www.onebillionrising.org

3.   UK Feminista:

A movement of ordinary men and women campaigning for gender equality. Lots of younger people are involved in this - the next generation of gender equality campaigners. Current campaigns include banning page 3 models and more stringent rules regarding images of women in lads magazines. They organise demonstrations, an annual summer school and email updates. It is completely free to join.

www.ukfeminista.org.uk

Further reading

Cochrane, Kira Women of the Revolution: *Forty Years of Feminism*, (London, Guardian Books, 2012)

De Beauvoir, Simone *The Second Sex*, (Middlesex, Penguin, 1972)

Forster, Margaret *Good Wives?* (Chatto and Windus 2001)

Furlong, Monica (ed.) *Mirror to the Church: Reflections on Sexism*, (London, SPCK, 1988)

Friedan, Betty *The Feminine Mystique* (London, Penguin, 1963)

Garner, Ralph *Josephine Butler: A Guide to her Life, Faith and Social Action*, (London, Darton, Longman and Todd, 2009)

Graham, Elaine. Walton, Heather and Ward, Frances *Theological Reflection: Methods*, (London, SCM Press, 2005)

Greer, Germaine *The Female Eunuch*, (London, MacGibbon and Kee Limited, 1970)

Hedges, Paul M. and Race, Alan (eds.) *Christian Approaches to Other Faiths*, (London, SCM Press, 2008)

LeGates, Marlene *In Their Time: A History of Feminism in Western Society*, (New York, Routledge, 2001)

MacCulloch, Diarmaid *A History of Christianity*, (London, Allen Lane, 2009)

Radford Reuther, Rosemary *Sexism and God-Talk*, (London, SCM, 1983)

Radford Reuther, Rosemary *Women – Church: Theology and Practice*, (New York, Harper and Row, 1985)

Slee, Nicola *Faith and Feminism: An Introduction to Christian Feminist Theology*, (London, Darton, Longman and Todd, 2003)

Slee, Nicola *Women's Faith Development: Patterns and Processes*, (Aldershot, Ashgate Publishing Limited, 2004)

Walters, Margaret *Feminism: A Very Short Introduction*, (Oxford, Oxford University Press, 2005)